My Practice Workbook

Writing and Punctuation

with Kids Club

Ages 7–9

This book belongs to: ....

I completed this book on

Date: ....

Signature: ....

Well done

HODDER Education

Advice for parents and carers

These days we are expected to be able to write fluently either by hand or on a keyboard, depending on the purpose of our writing. This book therefore gives lots of practice in writing activities, to help children think and plan, imagine and create through their writing. It can be daunting to start writing on a blank page, so these pages are devised to give your child the starting points and building blocks to get them writing. Extra paper should be available for longer writing tasks.

There is a whole range of writing forms represented in the book, from lists and adverts, through letters and playscripts, to short stories and poems. These are all forms of writing that children cover at ages 7–9: the first half of the book being non-fictional forms, and the second half fictional.

Practising and checking punctuation is deliberately integrated within the writing tasks, rather than being taught separately, out of context.

- On the left-hand side of each double page is a model of a particular form of writing, to remind your child of the style, layout and punctuation of that form.
- On the right-hand side is space for your child to write their own piece in a similar style. But encourage your child to use their imagination and think of their own content, characters and contexts for writing. These are 'open-ended' tasks, so that each child can write to their own level of ability.
- Each unit ends with a further suggestion for writing that your child can do away from the book.
- The book ends with a quiz, to round up what your child has learnt.
- And finally we provide answers, to help either parents and carers or children to check their work.
- The **'Tips from teachers'** are written by practising classroom teachers. They give useful advice on specific topics or skills, to deepen your child's understanding and confidence and to help you help your child.

Hachette UK's policy is to use papers that are natural, renewable and recyclable products and made from wood grown in well-managed forests and other controlled sources. The logging and manufacturing processes are expected to conform to the environmental regulations of the country of origin.

Orders: please contact Hachette UK Distribution, Hely Hutchinson Centre, Milton Road, Didcot, Oxfordshire, OX11 7HH. Telephone: +44 (0)1235 827827. Email education@hachette.co.uk Lines are open from 9 a.m. to 5 p.m., Monday to Friday. You can also order through our website: www.hoddereducation.co.uk

ISBN: 9781398388833

First published in 2013. This edition published in 2023 by Hodder Education, an Hachette UK Company, Carmelite House, 50 Victoria Embankment, London EC4Y 0DZ

Typeset and printed in the UK. Character illustrations by Lisa Hunt from the Bright Agency. Other illustrations by Fakenham Prepress Solutions. A catalogue record for this title is available from the British Library.

Impression number 10 9 8 7 6 5 4 3 2 1

Year 2027 2026 2025 2024 2023

Contents

Welcome to Kids Club!

Hi, readers. My name's Charlie and I run Kids Club with my friend Abbie. Kids Club is an after-school club that is very similar to one somewhere near you.

We'd love you to come and join our club and see what we get up to!

I'm Abbie and I run Kids Club with Charlie. Let's meet the kids who will work with you on the activities in this book.

My name's Jamelia. I look forward to Kids Club every day. The sports and games are my favourites, especially on Kids Camp in the school holidays.

Hi, I'm Megan. I've made friends with all the children at Kids Club. I like the outings and trips we go on the best.

Hello, my name's Jae. Kids Club is a great place to chill out after school. My best friend is Alfie – everyone knows Alfie!

I'm Amina. I like to do my homework at Kids Club. Charlie and Abbie are always very helpful. We're like one big happy family.

Greetings, readers. My name's Alfie! Everybody knows me here. Come and join our club. We'll have a great time together!

Now you've met us all, tell us something about yourself.

All the children filled in a '**Personal profile**' when they joined. There's one on the next page for you to complete.

Personal profile

DRAW A PICTURE OF YOURSELF HERE

Name: khadijah

Age: 7/8

School: st margrets ce primary

Home town: manchester

Best friend: sophia / ubah

My favourite:

✱ Book willy wonka,

✱ Film barbi,

✱ Food chiken strips,

✱ Sport football.

My hero is my mum because she loves me and she cares for me that wy

When I grow up, I want to be a face painter / meandy desiner.

If I ruled the world the first thing I would do is to have there own mantion for free.

If I could be any celebrity for a day, I would be a Mp because you ~~she~~ kan get rules from other people.

Write a list

Here's a list that Megan wrote. It lists all her favourite things in life. They are all the things she'd save if there was a flood!

My pink boots
My old teddy bear
My gran's photo
My first tooth
My black mouse
My diary
Big bottle of water for survival
My mobile
My purple pen
The chocolate cake from my last birthday party

Get ready

1 Do you use capital letters in this kind of list?

No

2 Do you use punctuation in this kind of list?

No

3 When do you start a new line in a list?

when you finish the line.

Tick the box when you complete the page. ✓

Let's practise

Now write a list of the ten things you'd save, if you knew a mega-disaster was coming!

Never mind if some of them are a bit difficult to pack . . .

1 My Money to keep safe.
2 whaker
3 bag of crisp
4 My Quran / spare
5 My birth day present.
6 purce
7 My Phone
8 My may cup
9 a tasbi
10 blanket

Have a go

Go and ask other people in your family what they'd save, and make lists for each of them.

Tips from teachers

There are no trick questions here! Just look at the list to answer questions 1–3 in **Get ready**. Will you pack things that you treasure or things that will help you survive? Use the example list to help your own writing.

Write a recipe

A recipe is a kind of **instruction**, which tells you how to make something.

It's often a recipe for cooking, but it might be for making something else.

Here's a recipe that's really different.

How to make your mum happy

<u>You will need:</u>

1 piece of card | 1 tray | Your mum's favourite food and drink

<u>What to do:</u>

1 Fold the card and draw a picture on the front.
2 Write a message inside, telling your mum what a great person she is.
3 Find a tray in the kitchen, or a very strong piece of board.
4 Pile on her favourite food and drink.
5 Find a good moment when she's sitting down.
6 Give her the tray and your card as a big surprise.
7 Last of all, give her a big kiss!

Get ready

What are the headings for the two parts of the instruction?

1 Decoration:

2 food:

Let's practise

Now think up your own idea for a recipe in life.

It could be how to make your best friend happy, or it could be how to make a really awful mess!

You will need:

decoration

food / drink

games

What to do:

1 you decorate youre houle with decor

2 you will have to make a present

3 set up food and drink on table

4 set up games for the fun to begin

Have a go

Write down the recipe for cooking your favourite food.

First list the things you need, then list the things you do to make the dish. Make your instructions as clear as possible.

Tips from teachers

Look back at the recipe you are given as an example on page 8 to help you come up with ideas and remember – there's no right answer. Just use your imagination!

Write directions

Another kind of instruction tells someone how to get somewhere.

This is called giving **directions**, and it helps if you have a map to work from.

Here are the directions that Little Red Riding Hood's mother gave her to reach her grandmother's house in the woods.

Leave the house behind you, and walk straight on for half a mile.
When you come to the big oak tree, turn right.
Walk on another half a mile until you come to the stream.
Cross the bridge, and turn left.
When you reach the ruined farm, turn right.
Grandmother's house is then straight in front of you.

Get ready

Draw a line on the picture to show where Little Red Riding Hood had to go. Start from the house at the bottom.

Let's practise

Write the directions that Grandmother would have given Little Red Riding Hood to get back home. That is, if she hadn't been eaten by the wolf . . .

behind the house on the brige behinde the tree then go home.

Have a go

Write directions for your best friend, telling him or her how to get from school to your home. You could draw a map as well, if it helps.

Tips from teachers

Look carefully at the picture. Then read the directions. Place your direction line for each part of the journey, in turn. Check that your direction lines start in the bottom left of the picture and end in the top right.

Write a definition

When do you use a dictionary?

A dictionary is really useful for checking your spelling, and for finding out what words mean.

The meaning of a word is also called a **definition**.

Read the definitions below. Fill in the word you think each definition is describing on the first line.

noun ____ a large monster with wings, that you read about in stories ____ dragons

noun ____ a very big piece of ice floating in the sea ____ iceburg

adjective ____ a word describing the taste of nuts ____ salty

noun ____ a person whose job is to fit and mend water pipes and taps ____ engenir

verb ____ to go backwards in a car ____ ~~fyverc~~ reverse

Get ready

1. Look up the words in your own dictionary. Which definition do you prefer: the one above or the one in your dictionary?
2. Now write **noun**, **verb** or **adjective** after each word. Your dictionary may tell you this.

Let's practise

Now try writing your own definitions for these words:

deckchair	it is some thing that you sit on outside.
haunted	some thing that might skare ~~to~~ humans.
magnet	some thing that can stick on metle.
nose	some thing that you can smell whith.
rise	some thing that lifts up.
sword	some thing that is sharp.
wand	some thing that is magical.

Have a go

Play a game reading definitions from the dictionary and asking your friends to guess what the words are.

Tips from teachers

Remember a **noun** is a naming word, a **verb** is a doing word and an **adjective** is a describing word. A **noun** can be a *person*, *place*, *thing* or *idea* and an **adjective** describes a noun!

Write an advert

How do you persuade someone that they'd like what you like?

You have to be very good with words to describe something so that you make someone else want to try it too.

Take your favourite food, for instance – how can you turn a yummy taste into the kind of description that makes your best friend beg for a bite?

When you've crunched
through the munchy bit,
And sucked up the softy bit,
The rich bit in the middle
Is the melting chocolate centre
Of the perfect chocolate doughnut.
It's a chocoholic's dream come true!

Get ready

Find a highlighter pen, and mark each word in the advert that really tempts you.

Let's practise

Describe your favourite food, and draw a picture, to make us all want a taste.

red hot chicken strips

delistos pizza

Have a go

Invent a new toy, and write an advert persuading parents or carers to buy it for their children. Draw a picture, too, if you like.

Tips from teachers

Remember to use exciting **adjectives**. Words like *yummy*, *scrumptious* and *delicious* might help! If you want to make your advert even better why not try some creative **verbs** and some **alliteration**? For example, Try ***munching*** this ***perfect*** pepperoni pizza!

Write a questionnaire

Do you like asking questions? If so, you could try writing a questionnaire for friends and family to fill in.

Here's one that Megan wrote, with the answers she got from her granny.

What is your name?	Granny Ross
What is your favourite food?	Baked beans
What is your favourite colour?	Purple
Where was your favourite holiday?	Wales
Who is your favourite singer?	Billy Fury
What is your favourite animal?	Giraffe
What are your favourite shoes?	My fur boots
What time do you go to bed?	Never before 10 o'clock

Get ready

1. List the question words used at the start of the sentences.

   What , Were and Who

2. What is put at the end of each question? question mark

3. What punctuation is used in the answers? to , is and are

Let's practise

Now write your own questionnaire, for your friends or family.

You could add lots of different questions, like: What is the earliest thing you can remember happening to you?

What is your name? mum
What is your favrot food? rice
What is your Dream contory? abu dabi
What is your favrot colour? wight
Who is your farrot child? khadijah
what is youre favrot book? mr fox
what is yore favrout flower?
rose What is your farrot drink? rubicon
What is favourite animal? rabitt

Have a go

Make copies of your questionnaire, if you can, so you can ask lots of different people to fill in their answers.

Tips from teachers

If you have difficulty coming up with questions for your questionnaire, use the example provided on page 16 to help you. And remember, make questions relevant for your audience. *What's your favourite bedtime story* might not be the best question to ask your gran!

Write a letter

When do we write letters? When we want to tell someone something, and maybe when we don't know someone well enough to telephone or text.

Have you ever written to an author, to tell them how much you like their book?

This is the letter I typed to Michael Morpurgo to tell him how much I enjoyed reading his book *Little Foxes*.

26 Sunny Terrace
Chelmsford CO5 9AH

26 August 2023

Dear Mr Morpurgo,

I'd like to tell you how much I enjoyed reading Little Foxes.

I found the whole book a wonderful story about nature, which made me feel really sad at times, as well as wanting to read on to the end.

The bits I especially liked were when Billy saved the swan and found the fox cubs.

Thank you for writing this book. I shall try to find more of your stories in our library.

Yours sincerely,
Amina Desai

Get ready

Can you find all these parts of the letter? Draw lines to link them to the text above.

1. Home address
2. Date
3. Greeting
4. Message
5. Ending

Tick the box when you complete the page.

Let's practise

Write a letter to your favourite author. Tell them which is your favourite book of theirs, why you liked the book overall, what your favourite bit was, and what you might read next.

3 gareld
ave
M85 9Z

B

29 July 2024

Dear mr Roldal

I'd like to tell you about

earli and the chockolat factory.

I liked evry bit of it expsily of

it so bye bye.

Have a go

Write a letter to your local library, asking them to stock a book you've really enjoyed.

Tips from teachers

Make sure you lay out your letter correctly. Include what you are asked to on page 19. Then, check what you've written! If you're writing to an author, you'll need to be extra careful with your spelling and punctuation.

Explain in words

I'm fascinated by how things are made, or how things get to where they are.

We often use pictures or diagrams to show how these things happen.

Can you see what the pictures below are telling us?

1

2

3

4

5

6

Get ready

1. Talk through what's happening in the pictures, as if the person you're talking to doesn't understand them.

2. Did you notice which tense you were using? Was it the present tense or the past tense?

Tick the box when you complete the page. √

Let's practise

Now write down your explanation in words.

Use the numbered stages to help you.

1 feeding grass to cows

~~milking the cows milk~~

2 milking the cows milk

3 ~~put~~ put it in truck then put in ~~factories~~ factories and make the cartens of milk

4 ~~stoor them in cartens and boxes to give them to oter pepole~~ sen them in stores

5 ~~It~~ put it ~~wibe~~ in frigesyn ~~friges and~~

6 ~~ten~~ then eat and dink with it.

Have a go

Write out the explanation of how something else is made.

Try drawing the pictures as well, if you can.

Tips from teachers

It might help you when it comes to **Let's practise** to look back at each picture and say out loud what each picture shows. For example, you might say *Cows eat grass* for picture 1. Then write this down.

Write a newspaper report

Do you ever read newspapers, to read **reports** of things that have happened?

If the report describes the events in the order that they happened, it is called a **chronological report**.

Look at the newspaper report below, which describes an escape from a zoo.

PYTHON ESCAPES!

Fear and panic swept the town of Marwick as a mountain python escaped from its cage.

The keepers first noticed it was missing at dawn, when they went round with morning feeds. They raised the alarm, and local police were given instructions on how to corner the snake, if anyone reported a sighting.

Early in the day the local school reported a possible sighting, but the zoo were not sure if they believed the stripy creature spotted in the playground really was the python.

Residents at an old people's home then thought they'd seen something slithery, but again it disappeared before the police could follow it.

In the end the zoo found the python in the farm area, where it had eaten all the rabbits and mice. So maybe it had never got out into the town at all.

Get ready

1. What tense is the main report written in, the past tense or the present tense? ______________________________

2. Can you spot all the words that mark the sequence of time (connecting words), at the beginning of each paragraph? Mark them with a highlighter pen.

Tick the box when you complete the page. ☐

Let's practise

Now write a newspaper report of a dramatic incident in your home town.

Use the past tense, and use connecting words at the beginning of each paragraph, to stress the sequence of time.

Have a go

Write a report for your school newspaper or school website, describing an event that happened at school.

Tips from teachers

Read the first sentence of each paragraph in turn. This will help you spot the ***time words***. Examples of such words are *then*, *first*, *at midday*, *next* and so on. If you are stuck for ideas in **Let's practise**, make something up!

Write your point of view

Suppose you wanted to respond to that newspaper article about the python escaping. Imagine you thought the zoo should think more about safety in your school and neighbourhood. Here's the kind of letter you might write.

Primrose School
Princess Road
Marwick MAR 6JL

1 October 2023

Dear Marwick Zoo,

We were worried to read in the local newspaper that one of your pythons might have escaped last week.

We kept thinking we'd seen it in the playground, so we were very scared.

We think it's important for the local neighbourhood to feel safe, so we hope that you have enough guards to make sure your animals don't escape.

We'd like to hear more about how your zoo is run.

Yours sincerely,
Class 4B

Get ready

1. Compare this letter with the one on page 18. Which features do this letter and the one on page 18 have in common?

____

2. What were the class worried about?

____

3. How did they make the letter end on a positive note?

____

Tick the box when you complete the page. ☐

Let's practise

Now write your own letter to the zoo, expressing a different point of view. Maybe you think they shouldn't be keeping pythons there at all. Make sure you lay out the letter in the same way as the one from Class 4B.

Have a go

Look through your local newspaper for reports that make you want to respond. Write a letter to the newspaper giving your point of view.

Tips from teachers

Remember, when you write your letter in response to the newspaper article on page 22, to be polite. At the same time as saying what you think, why not give reasons for why you think this?

Write a playscript

Do you know what a playscript is?

A **playscript** is how we write out the words that people speak in a play.

Look at this example, and read the different speeches out loud.

[*The* MAYOR *is sitting with his* COUNCILLORS.]

MAYOR: What on earth are we going to do? Our town is overrun with rats!

1st COUNCILLOR: There are rats in the cellars!

2nd COUNCILLOR: There are rats in the streets!

[*Enter a young man, dressed in red and yellow.*]

PIED PIPER: Please, sirs. I think I can help you.

MAYOR: How can you do that?

PIED PIPER: I know a charm that makes animals follow me.

MAYOR: And how do you do that?

PIED PIPER: I play on this pipe, and the animals follow.

MAYOR: That's wonderful! What should we pay you?

PIED PIPER: [*Modestly*] I'd like a thousand gilders, please.

MAYOR: We'll give you fifty thousand gilders, sir!

Get ready

Now match each of these features to the script above, by drawing lines to examples in the text.

1. Name of the person speaking, in capitals
2. Words the people say, in ordinary type
3. Stage directions, in square brackets and italics

Let's practise

Try writing a part of a playscript.

You could choose a well-known folk tale, like the one here. Or you could use a story you make up yourself.

Include all the features from the example opposite. You will need to continue on a separate piece of paper.

Have a go

Act out your playscript with a group of friends.

Tips from teachers

If you have difficulty coming up with ideas for your playscript, you could always base your script on something you have seen on television. With such a short script, it's best to stick to only two or three characters.

Punctuate speech

In the last unit, we looked at how to write speech in a play.

If you are writing speech in a cartoon strip or in a story, you do it differently.

Below, we're going to show you the same story of the Pied Piper, first as a cartoon, and then as a story.

The Mayor was sitting with his Councillors, and he was very worried.
"What on earth are we going to do?" he asked. "Our town is overrun with rats!"
"There are rats in the cellars!" said the First Councillor.
"There are rats in the streets!" echoed the Second Councillor.
At that point a young man came in, dressed in red and yellow.
"Please, sirs," he said softly. "I think I can help you."
The Mayor was amazed. "How can you do that?" he asked.
"I know a charm that makes animals follow me," said the Piper.

Get ready

When do you use speech marks to show the words people speak?

Mark with a tick (✓) or a cross (✗).

1 Playscript ☐ 2 Speech bubbles ☐ 3 Story ☐

Tick the box when you complete the page. ☐

Let's practise

Take the playscript you wrote on page 27.

Write it out as a story, using the model opposite for how to do the speech marks. Look at the model carefully – it's quite fiddly, putting the speech marks and the other punctuation in the right places. You will need to continue on a separate piece of paper.

Have a go

Draw the same conversation as a cartoon with speech bubbles.

Tips from teachers

Here's a useful tip for **Let's practise**: whenever a new person speaks, take a new line. Also, notice what has happened to the directions from the playscript in the story. Remember to do this with your own story.

Write a character sketch

Can you describe someone so that your reader can really picture him or her?

Can you make your reader either want to meet the person or run a mile?

You have to describe all the little details of what people look like and how they might behave, if you are to make your reader really believe in them!

Here is a **character sketch**.

> I saw someone walking their dog this morning.
>
> At least, first I just saw the dog-lead in the gap of our front hedge. So I started to imagine who was on each end of the dog-lead, before I caught a full picture of the two of them.
>
> It was the dog I saw first. He was one of those pit bull terriers who look rather scary, but are probably quite amiable really. He had big square shoulders, and rather turned-out feet.
>
> He was moving slowly, as if he was not out for a walk so much as ambling out to inspect the neighbourhood. He had slitty eyes, as if he hadn't quite woken up yet.
>
> So it wasn't such a surprise when the owner then appeared in the next gap of the hedge. He was slow on his feet too. And his toes turned out too. He wasn't menacing at all, more just a sleepy character who liked to look a bit more frightening than he really was. I then remembered that I'd seen them both in the park, the dog asleep on the ground with his legs splayed out, and the man asleep on a bench, in the middle of the afternoon.
>
> They left me thinking: which came first, the man or the dog?

Get ready

1. Read the character sketch, and use a highlighter pen to mark the bits you think the writer has done best.
2. Are there any words you don't know? Either try guessing what they mean, or look them up in a dictionary.

Tick the box when you complete the page.

Let's practise

Try writing your own character sketch of a dog and its owner. Really try to picture them in your head. Don't forget to use lots of details to describe their appearance, and what this suggests about how they might behave.

Have a go

Look for a photo in a magazine of someone whose life you'd like to imagine. Try writing a day-in-the-life of your character.

Tips from teachers

Having a picture of a person in front of you as you write a character sketch helps. Try this. Also, brainstorming some useful describing words on rough paper before you write your sketch will make your writing even better.

Describe a setting

Where do stories happen? Where would you like to make a story of yours happen?

You need to use lots of adjectives to describe your setting, so that your reader can picture it exactly.

Deep in a dark black space. Dank and dark, bleak and black. Is there any light at all? Yes, there's a piercing white light ahead: could it be the mouth of a cave, or the light at the end of a tunnel? It's a tiny relief compared with this overwhelming blackness, this damp chilling darkness, enveloping everything. What are the sounds? A drip of moisture from the roof, falling into a puddle in the rough ground underfoot. But otherwise there is just silence, leaving me nothing to hear, as well as nothing to see. Where on earth am I?

Get ready

1. Highlight all the adjectives in the description above.
2. Do you think the description is effective? ______________________

____

Tick the box when you complete the page. ☐

Let's practise

Now it's your turn to describe a setting. Will you make it obvious where it is? Or will you leave your reader guessing? Don't forget your adjectives, and think of all the senses you use: sight, hearing, touch, taste and smell.

____

____

____

____

____

____

____

____

____

Have a go

Again, try looking through a magazine, this time to find somewhere gorgeous you'd like to go on holiday. Describe what you think the place would be like.

Tips from teachers

A good way to start your description of a setting is *As I look around me I notice . . .*
Other sentence starts that might help are:
I hear . . .
The smell of . . . drifts towards me.
I stretch my hand out and feel . . .

Plan a story

Now you can start to plan a whole story, using your character in your setting. (Or choose a new character in a new setting.)

What's going to happen? You need a **beginning**, a **middle** and an **ending** to make your plot work. Look at the plan below.

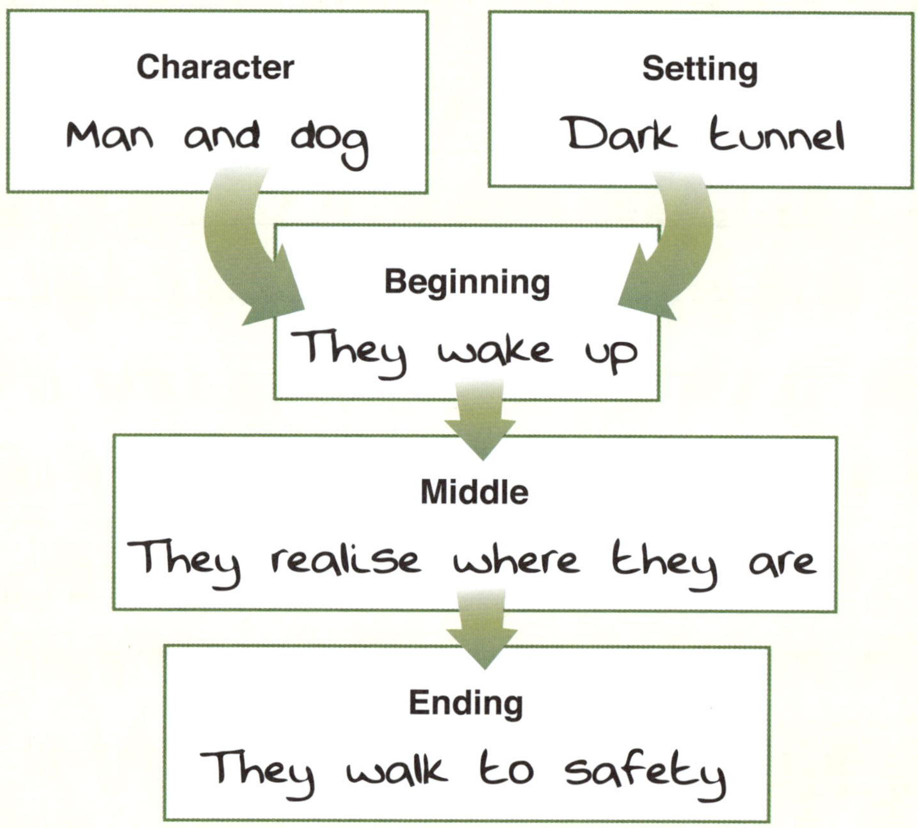

Get ready

Would you plan your character and your setting completely before you begin to plan your plot? Or do you think they might develop while you are writing?

~~we~~ when I write.

Tick the box when you complete the page. ✓

Let's practise

Fill in the boxes below to plan your own story.

When you come to write your story, you will write a paragraph each for the **beginning**, **middle** and **ending**.

Character

~~girl and boy~~ girl and cat

Setting

ocen ocean

Beginning

They Wake up and see that there ~~ia~~ is a crack ~~of water~~ in the ship.

Middle

More water creeps in the ship whil they set off.

Ending

They got to shore safly.

Have a go

When you are ready, get a separate piece of paper and write your story. This is just your rough draft. You will write your final version a bit later . . .

Tips from teachers

A good story plan will have a bit of drama in it. In the example plan the dark tunnel provides drama and excitement. Try to include some excitement in your plan too.

Punctuate your story

In the last unit we planned our stories, and you went off to write a rough version of your whole plot.

Here's what we wrote for the three paragraphs of our plot.

The man woke up slowly. Where on earth was he? It was pitch black, and rather damp. At least the dog was still at his feet; that was something. But what were they doing here?

He stroked his dog's familiar fur, to stop himself trembling with panic.

"Come on, boy," he said. "We've got to get out of here."

They headed towards the source of light, stumbling through the puddles.

"If only the dog could talk," he thought. "He could remind me how we got in here."

They headed forwards, the man keeping one hand on the side of the tunnel for safety. The shape of the light got bigger and bigger, in the shape of a growing white 'n'.

At last they broke into the daylight. They were on the bank of a little canal, which snaked round the hillside to bring water to all the crops. They had been inside one of the tunnels the canal flowed through, and the man must have fallen or passed out while they were in the tunnel. Never again! He would make sure he never walked through dark tunnels again for the rest of his life!

Get ready

When you've read the story, have a look at the punctuation.

1. Does every sentence start with a capital letter and end with either a full stop, a question mark or an exclamation mark? Underline them all.
2. Has the author used commas to separate a list, or to help the reader pause in the middle of a sentence? Mark the commas in blue.
3. Has the author used any semi-colons and colons in the middle of sentences for longer pauses? Mark them in pink.
4. Has the author used speech marks correctly for speech? Circle them.

Tick the box when you complete the page.

Let's practise

Now you can 'edit' your rough version of your story, by checking the four punctuation questions in **Get ready**.

When you are ready, copy out a final version of your story into the space below. You may need to continue on a separate piece of paper.

Have a go

Try writing a longer story, of more than three paragraphs. You could then make it into a folded book, with a proper cover, and give it to someone in your family as a present.

Tips from teachers

If you need some help with punctuation, you can always ask for help from a grownup. The most difficult bit will be punctuating speech. Look in books that you have read to see how this is done.

Write a different ending

Do you remember the setting and characters we brought together on page 35?

Well, maybe there's a different explanation of how the man and his dog got into the tunnel, and how they'll get out!

Here's a spider diagram with lots of different possibilities.

Get ready

Mark the spider diagram with ticks (✓), crosses (✗) and question marks (?) to indicate how you feel about each possibility.

Let's practise

Which option was your favourite?

Or would you choose something entirely different from your own imagination?

Write a different ending to the story, to make it more exciting for you. You may need to continue on a separate piece of paper.

Have a go

Take a well-known story, and write a completely different ending for it.

Does your ending make the story better?

Tips from teachers

When you **Have a go**, you could always try out a *funny ending* or an *unexpected ending*. Maybe you could even have a *mysterious ending*?

Write a poem

Write a whole poem myself! How scary does that sound?

Actually there are lots of ways of making it less scary. One way is to work from a 'model'. This means you look at the form or shape of someone else's poem, and use it as a 'prompt' to write your own. And that's quite all right – it's not cheating.

So, read aloud the poem below.

My Week at School

On Monday we did pottery,
On Tuesday we did craft;
On Wednesday we did sums and things,
On Thursday we just laughed.
On Friday we did question marks,
And What and Why and Who,
But now that it's the weekend
I can choose just what I'll do!

Get ready

Which lines rhyme? Number the lines, and draw lines to link the ones that rhyme.

Tick the box when you complete the page.

Let's practise

Try using the same idea, of the days of the week, to write your own poem.

Look out for which lines have to rhyme!

On Monday ______________________________

On Tuesday ______________________________

On Wednesday ______________________________

On Thursday ______________________________

On Friday ______________________________

____

____

____

Have a go

Try using times of day, or the months of the year, as a way of shaping some more poems.

Tips from teachers

Remember, a **rhyme** happens when the end sounds in two words sound the same. The words *see* and *three* rhyme. When you write your own poem, say lines aloud to help you rhyme them.

Write a shape poem

Do you like shape poems? I love reading them, but I've never tried writing one before.

One way of doing it is to draw the shape of a country or continent and then, inside the shape, write all the words that the place makes you think of.

Here's one on Australia, for instance.

Get ready

What colours does this poem make you think of? Colour in the shape with the right kind of colours.

Tick the box when you complete the page.

Let's practise

Now write a shape poem of your own. It doesn't have to be about a country; it could be about a food, or a building, or a person. Draw the outline shape first, and then fill it with words that the shape makes you think of.

Have a go

Write shape poems for a whole jungle full of wild animals!

Tips from teachers

There are a few colour words in the Australia poem which you may not know! Look up the words *terracotta*, *ochre*, *apricot* and *bronze* in a dictionary. When you write your poem, use a range of **adjectives**, **nouns** and **verbs**.

Write a haiku

Now let's try a **haiku**.

A haiku has three lines, with the middle line longer than the first and last.

Here are some examples.

a

An old pond
The sound of a frog jumping
Into water.

b

First day of school
Toes cramped and blistered red
From new school shoes.

c

Last day of term
Classroom chairs looking forward to
Weeks of peace.

Get ready

How many syllables are there in each line of the three haiku above? Many haiku have five, seven and five syllables in their three lines, but not all haiku follow this pattern.

Let's practise

Now try writing your own haiku.

Haiku are often about the seasons, so that might help to get you started.

Have a go

One author has recently tried condensing the plots of major novels into haiku. Could you do this for your favourite novel?

Tips from teachers

Remember a **syllable** is a one beat sound in a word. If you tapped out each beat in the word *tomorrow* (to-mo-rrow) you would hear that it has three syllables. The word *cramped* has only one syllable, however.

How have I done?

Quiz on writing

Can you remember which special features you'd find in these different kinds of writing?

Draw lines to match them up.

What you need:	Instructions
Turn left.	Character sketch
Address and date	Questionnaire
What's your name?	Speech
PIED PIPER:	Playscript
[*He came in slowly.*]	Recipe
"Too right," he said.	Directions
Poem of three lines	Setting
He was a burly man.	Haiku
It was a dark and stormy night.	Letter

Careful! It's not necessarily one feature per kind of writing . . .

Tick the box when you complete the page.

Quiz on punctuation

Each of these lines has an error of punctuation.

Write out the correct version on the line below.

1. "All right" said the clown.

____

2. I'll take all these the ball the ring and the crown.

____

3. The bird, which was sitting on the line sang the loudest.

____

4. How on earth can I handle all that.

____

5. "Are we going to school?" She asked.

____

6. William said. "It's just as well."

____

7. You take the shortest; We'll take the longest.

____

8. It's about time too, I replied.

____

9. Those were the days she said, with a sigh.

____

10. And that's all for now I'm afraid.

____

Tips from teachers

The **special features** are on the left and the **types of writing** are on the right.

To match the **feature** 'Turn left' in the left-hand column, draw a line to the **type of writing** 'Directions' in the right-hand column.

Answers

Pages 6–7
1 Yes, for each new line
2 No
3 For each new item

Pages 8–9
1 You will need:
2 What to do:

Pages 12–13
dragon, noun
iceberg, noun
nutty, adjective
plumber, noun
reverse, verb

Pages 16–17
1 What, Where, Who
2 Question mark
3 Only capital letter, no full stop

Pages 20–21
2 Present tense

Pages 22–23
1 Past tense
2 first, Early in the day, then, In the end

Pages 24–25
1 Address, Date, Greeting, Message, Ending
2 Their safety
3 Asking about how the zoo is run

Pages 28–29
1 Playscript (✗)
2 Speech bubbles (✗)
3 Story (✓)

Pages 32–33
1 Deep, dark, black, Dank, dark, bleak, black, piercing, white, tiny, overwhelming, damp, chilling, rough

Pages 34–35
Child's own answer

Pages 36–37
The man woke up slowly**.** **W**here on earth was he**?** **I**t was pitch black**,** and rather damp**.** **A**t least the dog was still at his feet**;** that was something**.** **B**ut what were they doing here**?**

He stroked his dog's familiar fur**,** to stop himself trembling with panic**.**

"Come on**,** boy**,"** he said**.** **"W**e've got to get out of here**."**

They headed towards the source of light**,** stumbling through the puddles**.**

"If only the dog could talk**,"** he thought**.** **"H**e could remind me how we got in here**."**

They headed forwards**,** the man keeping one hand on the side of the tunnel for safety**.** **T**he shape of the light got bigger and bigger**,** in the shape of a growing white 'n'**.**

At last they broke into the daylight**.** **T**hey were on the bank of a little canal**,** which snaked round the hillside to bring water to all the crops**.** **T**hey had been inside one of the tunnels the canal flowed through**,** and the man must have fallen or passed out while they were in the tunnel**.** **N**ever again**!** **H**e would make sure he never walked through dark tunnels again for the rest of his life**!**

Pages 40–41
Lines 2 and 4, and lines 6 and 8

Pages 44–45
a 3, 7, 4
b 4, 6, 4
c 4, 8, 3

How have I done? Pages 46–47

Quiz on writing

What you need:	Recipe/ Instructions
Turn left	Directions
Address and date	Letter
What's your name?	Questionnaire
PIED PIPER:	Playscript
[*He came in slowly*]	Playscript
"Too right," he said	Speech
Poem of three lines	Haiku
He was a burly man	Character sketch
It was a dark and stormy night...	Setting

Quiz on punctuation
1 "All right," said the clown.
2 I'll take all these: the ball, the ring and the crown.
3 The bird, which was sitting on the line, sang the loudest.
4 How on earth can I handle all that?
5 "Are we going to school?" she asked.
6 William said, "It's just as well."
7 You take the shortest; we'll take the longest.
8 "It's about time too," I replied.
9 "Those were the days," she said, with a sigh.
10 And that's all for now, I'm afraid.
or And that's all. For now I'm afraid.